DAVID & VICTORIA

AN INVITATION TO A WEDDING

DAVID & VICTORIA

AN INVITATION TO A WEDDING

JIM MALONEY

CONTENTS

INTRODUCTION 6

1

DAVID'S
STORY 8

2

VICTORIA'S
STORY 28

AT
HOME 48

3

THE
WEDDING 62

4

INTRODUCTION

As one of the world's most glamourous couples, David Beckham and his new wife Victoria, aka Posh Spice, have become used to living their life in the limelight.

Everything they do or say becomes news and barely a day passes without their pictures being in a magazine or newspaper. But how did they attain mega stardom at such an early age? What are they really like at home, away from the public glare? How do they plan to bring their baby Brooklyn up? These are some of the questions that this book attempts to answer, with exclusive interviews in their luxurious new apartment in Manchester.

And having been granted full and exclusive access to them at their wedding, you can read all about the preparations, how the big day unfolded and hear, in their own words, their thoughts and feelings as they make their most important commitment. All accompanied by glorious colour pictures.

In tracing their life stories it is interesting to find that they shared many similar qualities, even as children. Both were shy but overcame that by being fiercely ambitious and focussed on what they wanted in life – and that was fame. They were both star-struck at an early age. Victoria recalls seeing Barry Manilow on stage and said to herself, one day she'd be there too. At about the same time, David saw Manchester United play and coveted Bryan Robson's No 7 shirt.

*David and Victoria, Posh and Beckham –
however you know them, they have fast
become the most famous showbusiness
couple of the decade.*

Despite happy upbringings in close-knit families, both David and Victoria left home at 16 to follow their dreams: he to Manchester and United's training scheme; she to theatre college in Epsom. But it was also these good upbringings by supportive and sensible parents that has prevented them from becoming big-headed – even now that they have the world at their feet.

They are fondly remembered by many adults who helped them in their careers as being quiet, well-behaved youngsters. These are qualities that they now want to pass onto their baby son, Brooklyn.

Their focussed determination was even applied to their private lives. It was the reason they first began dating. David had seen Victoria performing in a Spice Girls video and told his United pal Gary Neville: "She's the one for me." And Victoria, who had heard that David liked her, says she, "Set out to get him!" and engineered a meeting with him in the players' lounge at Manchester's Old Trafford.

It wasn't long before they began attracting attention as a couple, notably for their sense of style and glamour, and they became the very epitome of youthful success – talent, money and good looks, as well as their evident devotion to each other. Having baby Brooklyn, they say, has made them feel complete.

So, as they embark on the next stage of their lives together, here's their story so far…

1

David Robert Joseph Beckham only ever wanted to play for Manchester United. His passion was passed on from his dad – a big fan of the club – who gave young David United's latest kit for Christmas every year. "We didn't have a lot of money, but we made sure that all three children got what they wanted. Where David was concerned, if he wanted a particular pair of football boots, then he got them, no matter how much they cost," his father now says.

Chapter 1

DAVID'S STORY
a football hero is born

Above

Footballer turned
model, David
shows off his
classic good looks.

The Manchester United star was actually born in East London, and later moved to Essex. His father Ted is a kitchen equipment fitter and mum Sandra, a hairdresser. He has two sisters Joanne and Lynne. David's proud of his cockney roots and, even today, loves pie and mash and jellied eels!

The football-mad youngster admits to being no great scholar, although his mum says he was a good artist. "He was always drawing cartoon characters. I've kept all his old sketchbooks," she says. "And he was very tidy and would make his own bed every day. Even now he can't stand mess." Ted adds: "He's the only fella I know who folds his dirty washing!"

Says David: "There were to be no academic qualifications for me. My mum wanted me to concentrate better on my school work and often chided me on my

Left

An eight-year-old David leaves Barcelona with other members of the Bobby Charlton Soccer School.

Right

Even as an excited child, David always found time to phone home and keep in touch with his parents.

Above

A young David proudly poses for a picture with one of his childhood heroes, Sir Bobby Charlton.

Below

David with another hero, Terry Venables, who was chief coach of the young team in Barcelona.

13

DAVID BECKHAM

"I left school on most afternoons with a football under my arm, wondering when the next kick-about would start."

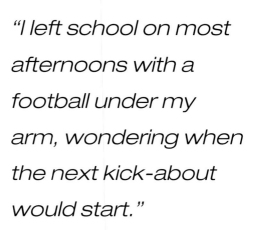

"All I ever wanted to do was play for Manchester United. There was never another team for me, from the time my dad took me to see them play at White Hart Lane."

reports, but both mum and dad knew that I wanted to be a footballer and, with a little bit of luck, that I had the talent to make it. I watched the likes of Bryan Robson, Gordon Strachan and Frank Stapleton in those wonderful red shirts. There were stars in my eyes and the club had taken a hold over me. The moment I saw Bryan Robson in the No 7 shirt I wanted to be like him – playing in colossal games in the biggest stadiums in the world and to wear the same shirt."

In his youth, David's dad played amateur football for Leyton Orient and Walthamstow. He later ran a Sunday league side and David would accompany him from the age of four. When the game was over, he and his dad would practise on the pitch together, kicking and shooting until late in the evening. "I knew he was good. He had things I'd never seen in a little kid before – he had crossing ability and control," says Ted.

David had no other ambition than to be a footballer and he was sure he would make it to the top, telling his dad that one day he was going to play for Manchester United. "I never thought of doing anything but play football. I used to tell everyone what I wanted to be and they would laugh and say, 'Yes, but what else are you going to do?' I would say, 'Just football.' When I needed to be somewhere for a trial, a match or anything else connected with the game, Dad was there to make certain I made it in time. When I wanted advice he was there, although in the end he always said it was up to me. With that kind of support behind me from the outset I have learnt to stand on my own two feet and not be afraid to make the right choices."

Sandra says: "We used to take lots of cine-films when David was little, and in every one, he's got a ball. We've got a

Left
David's good
looks led to an
advertising
campaign with the
hair product
Brylcreem.

Above
David, posing for a
natural-looking
portrait, in 1997.

film of him at 18 months, kicking his first ball, wearing a little Manchester United
strip! From the age of seven, he used to play in the park across the road, where I
knew he'd be safe. I had a friend who worked in the hut there, and I used to ring
and tell her he was on his way so she could keep an eye on him.

"He was never naughty – except for the time when he got his ears pierced at
14, without my permission! He'd asked me if he could do it, and I said no, because
it could be dangerous if he got his earring caught on something when he was
playing football. But he did it anyway. He came in the front door and ran straight
upstairs, so I knew something was wrong. I let him keep the earring in, but he soon
decided he didn't like it anymore and stopped wearing it."

He was keenly interested in his appearance at an early age as Ted remembers:
"He always dressed very well. Whenever he asked for clothes for his birthday or
Christmas, it had to be a designer name. He was always good-looking and quite

popular with the girls. He never went through an ugly duckling stage, although I remember him being self-conscious when he lost his teeth."

At school he was such a good footballer that he played for the year above his own. For his local club side, Ridgeway Rovers, he scored 101 goals in 115 games.

His big break came at the age of 11 when he was watching *Blue Peter* on television and heard about the Bobby Charlton Soccer Coaching School. There were going to be skill sessions across the country and the winners from the regions would have the chance to compete in the final at Old Trafford. To young David, it seemed too good to be true. Here was his golden chance.

"I raced in and asked my mum whether I could go in for it and she said I could," he says. "My grandad said he would pay the £125 it cost to enter.

Above
Being made a member of the England team was one of the proudest moments in David's career.

Right
David's success has made him a role model and spokesman for many young players.

How can I ever thank him enough? It was a defining moment in my life."

David made it to the final and halfway through the competition it was announced over the Old Trafford loudspeakers that he had won. "A wonderful moment," he now says.

At one stage it looked like he was going to be snapped up by Tottenham Hotspur – something which pleased his grandad, who was a big fan of the North London side. A scout came to watch Ridgeway Rovers and recommended David to Tottenham. He began training twice a week with the youth team at White Hart Lane. But he wasn't about to change his allegiance. "I got a lot of stick for turning up in my red Man United kit," he laughs.

David began playing for Waltham Forest Under-12s, whose coach recalls: "He had the best skills of any 12-year-old I'd ever seen." But David started to think that his beloved Manchester United would not be interested in him because he was in the south. Little did he know that his dream was about to come true. After one match his mum called him over and said: "It's lucky you had a good game because there's been a scout from Manchester United watching. He's going to call your dad later to discuss taking you to the club for trials." Says David: "Apparently I leapt in the air and started to cry!"

That scout was Malcolm Fidgeon, who recalls: "He was very frail and tiny, but he could do things the other boys couldn't and I thought he wouldn't disgrace himself if he was given the opportunity of a United trial. He never showed his emotions much but there was a touch of steel about him. For his size, David hit the ball extremely firmly but, more importantly, very accurately. At 12, he could take

Above

In 1998 Adidas chose David to represent them and their football boots.

Right

David took the sponsorship seriously and was keen to show the power of Adidas footwear in action.

corners on full-length pitches and hit the penalty spot. And he was very accurate from set pieces. Sometimes he got knocked off the ball because he wasn't big enough, but I was looking for a potential Manchester United footballer at eighteen or nineteen."

But, like David's dad, Malcolm couldn't help but notice that the lad was rather vain! "He was always last out of the training rooms. Even as a 12 year-old he was always gelling his hair," says Malcolm. But Malcolm was struck by his good manners. "When we drove up to Manchester, David was very polite. In fact, years later England Under-21 boss Ray Wilkins remarked that if he had a daughter, David was the sort of lad he'd like her to date. That sums him up."

David left Chingford High aged sixteen and joined United's training scheme, living in lodgings and seeing his parents at weekends. Showing typical determination, he set to work on strengthening his body. Says Malcolm: "He would stay behind after training and use weights to build himself up. On top of that he enjoyed very clean living. He would be in bed by 9pm and was not distracted by the pull of pubs and clubs."

Being away from friends made him focus on his football. "People have asked me whether I missed going down the pub with my friends when I was 16, but I was doing what I wanted to do. I'd much rather stay in on Saturday night and watch *Match of the Day*, because I had a game on Sunday."

David's mum recalls: "He didn't do much reading but he'd read former Man United captain Bryan Robson's autobiography, in which Bryan said he drank a raw egg mixture to help build his strength. So he did that for a while." A year later, the rather fragile youngster was much bigger.

As a trainee apprentice, he would be one of the first at the training ground every morning, cleaning boots and sweeping the floors. But he was clearly destined for greater things - and he was in a hurry. Just a year after leaving home, he helped United's youngsters secure the FA Youth Cup. He also forged a lasting friendship with Gary Neville, who was in that team. They climbed the rungs together to both the Manchester United A-team and the national side. And Gary was to become David's best man at his wedding.

David went on to play for United Reserves and had a brief spell on loan to Preston before being picked for Manchester United's senior team. "My dreams had finally come true," he says. His proud parents watched him play at all the home and away games and continue to do so. But there was greater glory to come.

David caught everyone's attention – including that of England coach Glenn Hoddle – with an astonishing goal for United from inside his own half against Wimbledon in 1996. His soaring shots and precision passing eventually prompted Hoddle to put him in the England World Cup qualifier against Moldovia. David's life was taking on that of every boy's fantasy.

With United he surpassed all his dreams by winning the historic treble – the FA Cup, Premiership and European Championship. David's parents' home now contains dozens of trophies and photographs of their son in footballing action.

The speed of his phenomenal success has surprised even David. And he admits that it's sometimes scary. "Everything has come so fast it frightens me," he says. And he understands how it causes resentment in some people. "Sometimes people think I should be struggling more, but they don't understand that there's a lot of pressure

Right
Playing the World Cup qualifier at Wembley in November 1996.

21
DAVID
BECKHAM

at a club like United, with plenty of younger kids coming through. You can't afford to have a bad game," he explains.

With success has come considerable wealth and he is a great one for flashy cars – like his £200,000 Ferrari – and designer clothes. Gucci suits and Prada T-shirts are big favourites. And who will ever forget the sight of him in that Jean Paul Gaultier sarong? Companies besiege him with sponsorship proposals. With his talent, fame, youth and model-good looks, he is a marketing man's dream commodity. "I'd be lying if I said I didn't like nice clothes," he says. "I do enjoy shopping and if I really like a pair of trousers, there isn't any limit to the price I'd pay. And I've never looked at a car and thought: 'That's too much money, I can't

spend that.' I love cars. I suppose I'd pay anything really. But I haven't lost the value of money. I'm not the sort of person who doesn't look at price tags. I'm always quite careful with money." (Although Victoria may disagree!)

Does he ever think he's paid too much? "I gave up a lot when I was younger – going out with the lads to parties and discos, leaving my family to move to Manchester," he reasons. "It wasn't easy, but I knew what I wanted to do. I knew my place was at Manchester United. There's a lot of money made in the game so I don't think there's anything immoral about what I make as a result."

Having set his heart on Manchester United, he turned next to other matters of the heart. "I was abroad with the England team. Gary Neville and I were in the hotel room and a Spice Girls video came on," he says. "I pointed at the screen and told him: 'That's the girl for me and I am going to get her.' It was her eyes, her face. She's my idea of perfection. I was sure just from seeing her on that video that she was the one I wanted and I knew that if she wanted me we would be together forever. It didn't go exactly to plan at first but fortunately she felt the same way."

They met when she came to watch him play but he was so nervous that he barely spoke to her! Luckily, she paid another visit and this time he managed to ask her for a date. "I fancied her like mad but I didn't want to rush things," he says. "It was hard but I managed to stop myself kissing her until our fourth date. I'm glad I waited. It was a great kiss."

Busy careers mean that they spend a lot of time away from each other but they stay in touch. "We spend a small fortune on phone calls," says David. "The club

23
DAVID
BECKHAM

"Alex Ferguson summoned me to tell me that I'd been chosen for England. My heart began to race, I was so proud."

Left
Proving his worth as part of the England team in the World Cup in France, 1998.

Right
Again playing for the national team – this time an International Friendly at Wembley, 1998.

physiotherapist said I may have slightly damaged my neck because I've spent so much time cradling the phone on my shoulder. And he wasn't joking!"

Ted and Sandra weren't sure what to expect when their son told them that he was dating a Spice Girl. Says Ted: "Of course, we knew who the Spice Girls were, but we didn't know much about them." Sandra adds: "The first time Victoria came round for dinner, we did think: 'Oh, a pop star. What's she going to be like?' But she was just very normal, and we liked her straight away."

When David proposed to Victoria in a Cheshire hotel, he says he suddenly got a pang of nerves. "I'd bought the ring and was really looking forward to it. But when the moment came there were a few butterflies. It was very funny when she pulled out a ring for me too. Typical!" he laughs.

David's parents were delighted when Victoria became pregnant. Says Sandra: "David told us in Manchester, face to face. Victoria was on tour at the time. We were pleased, but a bit shocked, like most mums and dads would be. But I knew that David would be a good dad because he's always liked children. As soon as my daughter Lynne had her baby, he came home that same day, and he was very good when his younger sister Joanne was born."

After the infamous red card incident when David was sent off for kicking an Argentine footballer in the World Cup, mum and dad were on hand to to comfort him. "We went up to him right after the game and cuddled him," says Ted.

David says it was a learning experience. "Being sent off

Right

Showing the FA
Cup to United fans
in a triumphant
parade through
Manchester's
streets in 1999.

Left above

Gary Neville and
David, after winning
the Premiership
title in 1999.

Left below

David proudly
sporting his medal
after winning the
Premiership title.

and having to cope with the flak I received made me grow up," he says. "I think I learned about my personality, and about stress. My United boss, Alex Ferguson, helped me a lot, too."

Becoming a father has also put things into perspective. David held Victoria's hand when she gave birth by Caesarean section to their son Brooklyn at London's Portland Hospital. "I cried when he was born. I wanted to cut his umbilical cord, but the doctor did it so quickly I didn't get the chance," he says. "Brooklyn's got Victoria's nose and colouring but he's starting to go blonde like me. He's got my legs, my feet and my toes. Being a father is just how I expected it would be. I knew I would enjoy it. It's just unbelievable that someone comes out of a person who you love so much, like I love Victoria.

"Having a baby has made me grow up, too. Football's not the only thing in my life any more. He's made me look at life from a new perspective. Things that were important before just don't seem as important now that I have Brooklyn and Victoria. We're a family now and I'm the happiest I've been in a long time. If something winds me up at work I come home and take one look at what we've made together and everything else just seems... I can't really put it into words. It's strange because I've become so attached to him that it's hard for me to think about anything else. I don't think it has really affected my game because I am still enjoying my football, but I am also thinking about my little boy and Victoria all the time, every minute."

Not only is David a proud father, he's very hands-on too. "Victoria has been breastfeeding so when he cries she has got up to feed him but I always wake up as well and I give him a bottle sometimes so she gets a rest. We had a child so that we can raise him – not a nanny. And I do my fair share of changing nappies! It's great looking after him. It does tire you, but we're not as tired as everyone has been saying. We are both loving it; this is the best time of our lives.

"Brooklyn's doing great. I hope that we are going to be just like any other

"I've learned certain things about the game and outside of it too."

parents. It really doesn't matter that we are famous. We are going to love him and look after him, and we are going to be strict as well. Victoria is adamant about that. We can't stand those naughty little kids who run about in restaurants. He's going to be a well-behaved little boy. I think about him and his future, and we've got all these hopes for him, but whatever he wants to do, as long as he's happy, then we will be happy.

"Victoria will keep going with her career and that's something we are both really happy with. Some nights we will have time apart because of our careers but we won't be apart for too long.

"I'm looking forward to the future. You know, there's always something to aim for. A lot of players would like to go into management or coaching, but I would like to start a soccer school like the Bobby Charlton school that I loved so much. I would like to do it for boys and girls of all ages. I'm still young. It's usual to retire at around 35 or 36, and I'd like to play for as long as I can because it is something I will always enjoy."

Above
Playing for England again, in the Euro 2000 qualifier games against Poland and Sweden.

Right
Holding up the FA Cup for the fans, moments after winning the prize.

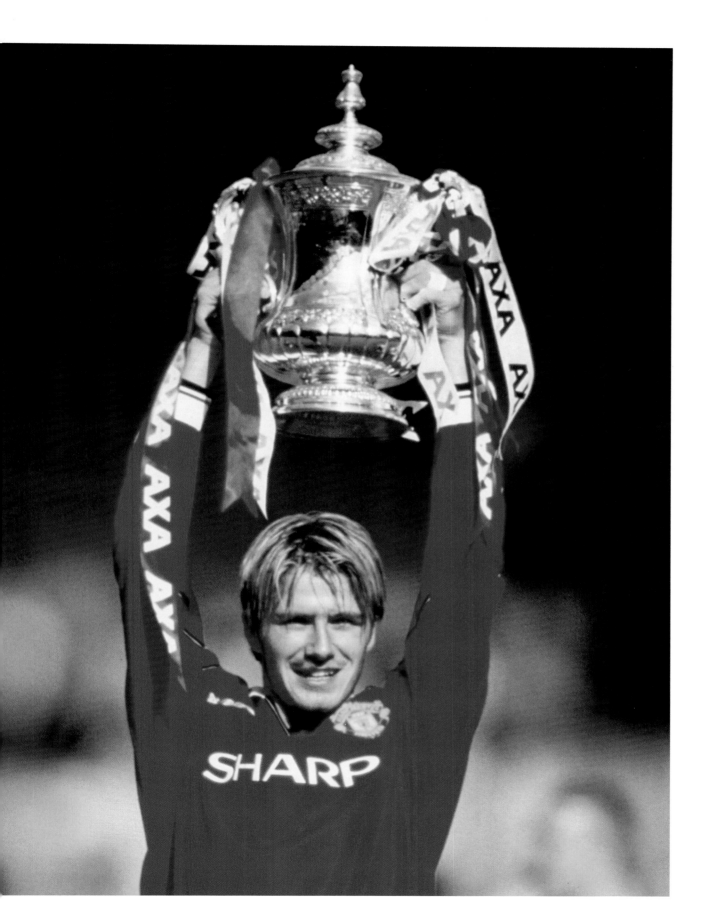

Victoria laughs at her Posh label, but she did have a privileged upbringing, enjoying the luxury of her parents' sprawling house in Goff's Oak, Hertfordshire, complete with swimming pool, nice holidays and cars. But, she says, "The only way I might be said to be spoiled was that I was given too many hugs, and that just made me affectionate."

Chapter 2

VICTORIA'S STORY
a Spice Girl is born

Above

Calm and poised, Victoria is at the high point of her career and personal life.

Victoria is the eldest of three children from a close-knit family, and has a sister, Louise, and brother Christian. But she wasn't the first in her family to try her hand at showbusiness – her dad was in a band called The Sonics in the 1960s, before she was born. But star struck at an early age – she took dancing lessons from the age of three –Victoria admits to being a show-off. "I had one of those wrap-around skirts like the girls in Bucks Fizz wore in the European Song Contest and I used to whip it off in the playground at school and say: 'Everyone watch me!'"

Former teacher Sue Bailey at her primary school, Goff's Oak Junior Middle and Infants, recalls: "Victoria was such a pleasant child, very pretty, not at all pushy. I can remember her in the leading role of *The Pied Piper*. She was keen on drama."

From there she went to the local secondary school, St Mary's High in Cheshunt. But envious school colleagues made her life difficult, and it didn't help that her dad

Tony, who runs an electrical distributions company, dropped her off at school in his gold Rolls Royce! "I used to beg to go in the van," she recalls.

Victoria's schooldays were not happy ones. In fact, there were often times when she dreaded going to school, fearful of the bullying she would receive. "I was one of those kids who was really boring and I used to work hard when the cool thing to do was to have a cigarette behind the bike sheds and be snogging whoever – but I wasn't into that. My parents had brought me up the way they thought was proper and I never used to swear, so I wasn't very popular."

General resentment took a particularly nasty turn in that spiteful way that schoolchildren are particularly adept at. "I remember I'd go to classes and be petrified. I'd usually get pushed around and sworn at, and they'd threaten me with remarks like, 'We're gonna get you after school.' Later on, they'd be waiting for me at the school gates and start pushing and pulling me. For a while I was a complete wreck. I would wake up worrying about who I was going to go out with at lunchtime and who I was going to sit with in class. I'd feel sick at the thought of school. I can't explain how horrible being bullied made me feel. It was pure hell."

But it was to be a character-building experience that gave her the strength to

Below

Victoria (front row, left) backstage in the show *Bertie* at the Alexandra Theatre in Birmingham in 1993.

Above

"Posh Spice",
along with the
other Spice
"characters" was
an idea that came
from the girls
themselves.

rise above such taunts. She explains: "When I got older my attitude changed and I started to think, 'To hell with you, I'll have my day.' And after a while kids realised it wasn't getting to me, so they didn't bother anymore." And anyway, Victoria was sure that one day her life would change beyond all recognition.

Now one of the most glamorous women in the world, it's hard to believe that boys took no interest in her at school. "My younger sister Louise had loads of friends and boyfriends and was always very popular, and I suppose I was a bit jealous of her," she admits. "At one stage I didn't really have any friends, so I used to hang around with Louise and her friends. I was always too embarrassed to have a boyfriend. No one fancied me anyway. I was more interested in clothes."

Victoria took an early interest in her appearance and clothes – a trait that has remained with her, now she can afford the best of designer wear. But she has always made the best of herself, whatever the circumstance. She may have dreaded school but that didn't mean she shouldn't look her best – Victoria used to get up two hours before school to do her hair and make-up! "I've always been bothered about my appearance," she says. "I used to wear make-up to school and as soon as I got home I'd be told to wash it off."

That scene in *Spiceworld – The Movie*, in which a preened Posh, in mini-skirt and heels, turns her nose up at army fatigues, has a ring of truth about it. "I didn't do PE at school because I thought it would mess up my hair," she says. "My mum used to write me a note saying that I'd been injured." School uniform need not be dull, when you have an eye for fashion. "We had a choice between a kilt and a grey skirt. I went for the grey one in a small size so it fitted me like a pencil skirt."

Ever the dreamer, Victoria made up for her lack of boyfriends by fantasising about Bros star Matt Goss, at that time, along with his brother Luke, the biggest thing in pop. "I was a real Bros fan and had stars and stripes jeans like the ones they wore," she says. "I remember screaming and going absolutely mental at one of their concerts because I was convinced I was going to marry Matt Goss. I was so obsessed. I went crying to my mum: 'I've got to meet him. You've got to tell me a way to meet him.'" She also recalls being taken along to a Barry Manilow concert by her mum, watching him on stage and thinking: "I want to be up there."

Victoria eventually went to theatre college in Epsom at age 16 but she admits that it was tough for her to shine there. "It wasn't easy because I wouldn't say that

Above & right

Victoria adopted a stunning new image when the Spice Girls attended the MTV awards in 1997.

35
VICTORIA
ADAMS

36
VICTORIA
ADAMS

I have natural talent," she says, with typical candour. "I wasn't the best and I was never picked for auditions. I worked hard but it was a struggle. Some of the teachers used to say to me, 'You'll never make it,' or 'You don't look right.' It was because I didn't have long legs, blonde hair and a natural acting ability. But there were others who encouraged me."

After a three-year course, Victoria joined the cast of a small-time touring musical company. Then she answered an advert in a newspaper to join a boy-girl band called Persuasion. She sent off her details and picture and, although she admitted that she hadn't sung professionally before, they thought she looked perfect, had great potential and were impressed by her keenness.

But within a few months of joining, in the summer of 1993, she read another advert, looking for "attractive dancers and singers" to form a five-girl band called Touch. She secretly contacted them and was one of the first to audition, along with two other girls – Melanies Brown and Chisholm. Victoria looked slinky in a figure-hugging crop top and black trousers and impressed the judges. She stayed with Persuasion for just over a year before getting a call from the Touch management, saying they were ready to launch and wanted her in the band. Victoria knew it was

Below
The girls surrounding HRH Prince Charles with their own brand of "Girl power".

"*This is some-thing I have always wanted to do. We are all working really hard and are really ambitious.*"

Left
Victoria was thrilled
when the girls had
the chance to
meet ex-President
of South Africa,
Nelson Mandela.

39
VICTORIA
ADAMS

Right
The Spice Girls
proudly show off
their Brit Award in
1998, proving their
worth in the music
industry.

"There is a lot more to me than the moody cow who just points and wears a short skirt."

the right move and it proved to be a major, life-changing decision. "When I knew I'd been successful, I told Persuasion that I didn't want to be with them any more. They reacted badly, shouting at me down the phone," she recalls. "But it wasn't a dilemma for me to decide because the new band seemed a lot more organised."

The other successful applicants were Emma Bunton and Geri Halliwell. When they had all teamed up, they lived together for a while. Victoria, the quietest one, sometimes found the exuberance of the others a little over the top. She recalls: "Geri was scatty with a very friendly nature and I remember thinking Mel B was really loud but I also thought: 'You are beautiful. Absolutely beautiful.' It was a fun time, but also difficult. We did have arguments, and I guess to begin with I did think, 'I come from a different background from the others,' but that quickly evaporated."

Left & right
Victoria's classic
beauty shines
through in even
the most abstract
images.

Spending so much time with the girls helped bring Victoria out of her shell.
But she was always the most sensible one. "When I first met the girls they used to
leap on tables and dance about. I was the only one who said, 'I don't know if we
should do that, because the table might collapse.' But they brought out another,
more fun side to my personality."

As Touch they performed in front of talent scouts and made a video in which
they talked about their hopes and ambitions of stardom. Touch evolved into the
Spice Girls when the original manager was replaced by Simon Fuller, and they were
on course for a level of success that even surpassed Victoria's wildest dreams.

Their debut single "Wannabe", stormed its way to Number 1, where it
remained for six weeks, their album *Spice* also topped the charts and "Girl power"

Left
Dressed to kill in a
Ruti Duan dress,
while on tour in
America.

"When I used to go shopping I'd dream about there being books with my name on. Now it's actually happened."

Above

Even in the early days of her pregnancy, Victoria was keen to show off her figure.

became a national catchphrase. Smooth marketing provided each girl with an image – Scary Mel B, Sporty Mel C, Baby Emma, Ginger Geri and Posh Victoria.

Victoria is amused by her moniker."Everyone thinks of me as that moody cow," she laughs. "I'm supposed to strut this sophisticated pose but I'm actually a real smiler. I don't mind being called Posh Spice, it's just a nickname. Actually it makes me laugh, and I suppose there is an element of me that is posh, in the sense that I like nice clothes and I'd prefer to go out to a really nice restaurant than go to a club. But I don't have a posh accent." Belying her sultry image, Victoria has a great sense of humour. She's down-to-earth and doesn't take herself too seriously.

"The day the Spice Girls got to Number 1 with "Wannabe", I rang my parents only to hear a mad party going on in the background. They had heard about it on the television and were all yelling: 'Congratulations! You're Number 1!' At the time I was in Japan on tour. I was lying in bed on my own and suddenly felt really depressed. I started crying because I wanted to be at home with them."

Victoria has always been very close to her family and, even today, she speaks to her mum every day on the phone. In one room of her parents' house, there is a wall completely covered with framed magazine covers of Victoria and the Spice Girls. "Mum is fantastic when I'm feeling down. She's always told me to stick it out and carry on," she says. "I've always had a good relationship with all my family, they cope very well with my fame. I sometimes feel bad that I'm a bit grumpy with them when I've been working hard. But I really love to spend time with them."

Louise now acts as her personal assistant but Victoria admits that there was a time when, like many sisters, the two of them would bicker. "We never physically fought, but it really upset my mum and dad because we'd argue all the time over absolutely everything and we couldn't bear the sight of each other," Victoria laughs. "Now she's probably my best friend. We share a lot of things and go out together whenever we can."

After "Wannabe" came the follow-up, "Say You'll Be There", and by 1997 the Spice Girls had had four number ones and were the first British group to conquer America with a debut single.

Victoria has had her fair share of critics in her life – usually stemming from jealousy – but she never forgets those who supported her. So it was that she invited two teachers from her drama college to the Spice Girls concert at Wembley in 1997. "They had encouraged me and I wanted them to see that I had made it in the end. After the show they winked at me and that just said it all for me."

At an all-time high, the girls crammed in as much as they could, including a lighthearted, celebrity-packed feature film called *Spiceworld - The Movie*. This was followed by a world tour in 1998.

In between, Victoria managed to find love –
with a certain footballer named David Beckham.
Two stars at the height of their fame was a match
made in showbusiness heaven. She had seen him in
a magazine and orchestrated a meeting in the
players' lounge. The Spice Girls were issued VIP
tickets to a Manchester United game against
Sheffield Wednesday and Victoria and David met
after the match. After a shy and hesitant start, they
began dating.

45
VICTORIA
ADAMS

Left
Exuding glamour
and style, dressed
by William Hunt and
Dolce & Gabbana.

"I knew he liked me but for the first three dates he wouldn't even kiss me," she says. "He finally got round to it when we were at my parents' house after our fourth date. It was worth the wait!" Although she'd had other boyfriends, the feelings she felt for David were such as she'd never experienced before. "I'd had previous boyfriends and even thought I was in love before but I was wrong," she says. "Falling in love with David made me feel complete. For the first time in my life I was happy – sincerely happy. David feels the same way. I'm more relaxed now. And I think I've made David more confident."

"I'm not Posh Spice to David and he's not a famous soccer star to me." In fact, when she watches him playing football, she feels it is a different person from the one she lives with. "It's almost like there's two different Davids – the one on the pitch and the one I'm in love with. Generally speaking, though, I never fancy footballers and I wouldn't have fancied any of the others. Actually when I first met David my mum said, 'Oh no, dear, don't go out with a footballer!'"

But Victoria knew she'd found the man of her dreams. "When I was in America we decided that we would get engaged when we got back home," she says. "We'd already looked at a few rings but I didn't know which one he had chosen. I'd told him what my dream ring would be. He remembered and had it specially designed for me. We spent a weekend in a hotel in Cheshire and ordered dinner and champagne in our room. We were sitting there in our dressing gowns when David pulled out the ring, got down on one knee and said: 'Will you marry me Victoria?' I said 'Yes' then produced my own ring and said: 'Don't forget Girl Power - will *you* marry *me*?'"

"I feel like I know what's important in life now – and it's not getting a discount at Gucci! I'm more relaxed now."

That feeling of completeness that they both have was reinforced when Victoria became pregnant. She gave birth to a baby boy at London's Portland Hospital on 4 March 1999. Victoria had an emergency Caesarean after doctors discovered that the baby was in the wrong position. They named their son Brooklyn, because he was conceived in New York. A delighted David bought her a £40,000 Mercedes as a present for giving birth!

Victoria is determined that their fame will not get in the way of raising Brooklyn in as normal a way as they can. They are caring for him themselves, without the help of a nanny. Wherever Victoria is working, Brooklyn goes with her.

"I don't want my children to be photographed all the time. I want my baby to have as normal a childhood as possible," she says. "We are both very normal. We do our own cooking. We do our own cleaning. We go out and drive ourselves. If I were to think, 'I'm famous, David's famous,' I'd just go mad. I think it's great that we've both got these jobs, but at the end of the day we shut the door and then we're who we are. We can sit in a room and talk for hours. We don't have the television on, we don't look at a magazine, a video. We can sit there and talk and talk. People don't know about that. They think all we do is go shopping and buy Gucci."

So what does the future hold for her professionally? "We all know the Spice Girls aren't going to last forever. We are optimistic but realistic. I want to act. Maybe as a Bond girl or something." But she's devoted so much time and energy to being a Spice Girl it's not something she wants to give up just yet.

Left

"I know what I want, I know what I want to achieve and I can speak up for myself!"

T hrough winding tree-lined turns of an affluent suburb on the the edge of Manchester, one arrives at electric gates that swing silently open, along a short drive which curves steeply up to a handsome 100-year-old apartment block. David and Victoria have taken the penthouse here, marked not by a discreet card by the entryphone, but by a goal-sized portrait of the couple which hangs in their entrance hall.

Chapter 3

At Home

David and Victoria together

Above

The relationship
between David
and Victoria is
openly affectionate
and loving.

Thick church candles flicker on high stands either side of their doorway. Dozens more are scattered through the spacious living areas: the kitchen with its fake leopard print scatter rug, stylish vertical radiators like ladders to the ceiling, and vast Miele oven; the bathroom with its enormous family bath, double shower and matching his and hers Versace towels and robes in black and gold; and the lounge with its four-foot elephant – a Christmas present from Victoria's mother – and low carved tables which support a selection of Buddhas and statuettes. The entire apartment is white with beautiful pale wood floors – not a million miles from the loft apartments in *Friends* and *Frasier*, the couple's favourite TV programmes.

It centres on a wide connecting hallway lined with black and white pictures of the Spice Girls on tour, David lining up for his opening game of the World Cup and an extraordinary portrait of Eric Cantona, dressed as a Roman Emperor,

Above

The couple attract attention wherever they go, whether shopping in London or jetting around the world.

Right

David and Victoria announced their engagement in January 1998, showing their joint diamond rings to the world.

surrounded by David Beckham and his Manchester United team-mates posed with suitably austere expressions. At the end of the hallway a silver star set in a door announces "Brooklyn's Room", the toy-cluttered first residence of their beloved baby boy who is sleeping peacefully on David's lap.

They may find themselves in the spotlight but Victoria is determined to guard Brooklyn's privacy. "I feel really protective of him," she says. "When I was in hospital I didn't see all the people that were outside and all the media and all the fans. I was just in there in my own little world – with Brooklyn – and it was lovely. I had the best week of my life."

She gives a slight frown. "Mind you, I did see a lot of newspapers saying that I was selling pictures of him. Brooklyn won't do any pictures until he is big enough to decide for himself that's what he wants to do or doesn't want to do. He's not a

"I knew from early on how strongly I felt for David."

53
DAVID &
VICTORIA

Above
Fast cars and
designer clothes
are passions of the
couple.

GUCCI

money-making venture for us." David looks up from Brooklyn and says: "I think we've accepted in our own lives, that we're not going to get much privacy, but as a family that's all we want now." The doting father admits he finds it difficult being away from his son when he's playing football or training. "I just want to spend every minute of the day with him, to see every little new movement he makes," he says.

The night Victoria went into labour, David was on his way to her parents' home in London to take her out for dinner. She called him to tell him they would have to cancel. "I felt sick as soon as she told me. I panicked because I was so nervous. I just wanted Victoria and the baby to be all right. Victoria was brilliant, really calm – not like me."

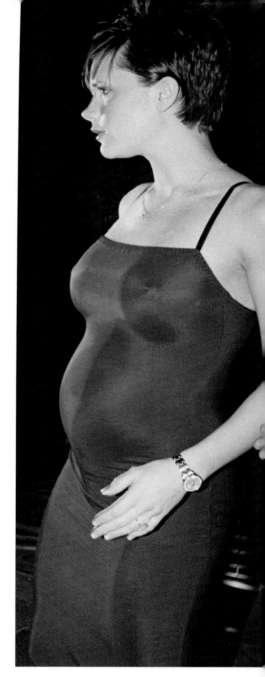

At London's Portland Hospital, things moved swiftly. Victoria recalls: "The baby's head was not in place and so I had a Caesarean, which was all very last minute. You have a choice – you can go into labour, but if the head still doesn't go into place you end up having an emergency Caesarean, which can make the baby stressed. All I was interested in was having a healthy baby, and it's funny how suddenly your mind begins to work and all your priorities change. When I was actually in the theatre, I said to David 'If they take the baby away, for whatever reason, just leave me here – half dead or whatever – and go with the baby. Make sure you don't let him out of your sight.' But all the doctors and staff were fantastic. Mr Gillard, who was the man who actually delivered Brooklyn, was brilliant. You can't even see my scar!"

David became very emotional. "Because it was a Caesarean I couldn't watch the actual operation, but Mr Gillard said: 'The head's halfway out, look.' I watched him pulling Brooklyn's head out, he opened his eyes and it was unbelievable. I just cried."

Says Victoria: "I was starving, because I hadn't eaten for hours, and I do eat a lot. So I was lying there, totally conscious throughout the operation – couldn't feel a thing – and moaning to David: 'I want some food.' My mum was in there as well – she videoed it! Not the whole thing but she videoed me being stitched up. I remember looking up and hearing my mum say, 'Smile!' She collects everything about me, she's got maybe 75 picture albums full of our newspaper cuttings and a video library of everything we've done on television."

Baby Brooklyn proved to be as hungry as mum. "The first thing he did, apart from scream, was open his mouth because he wanted feeding, and he took to breast-feeding straight away," says Victoria.

A couple of nights before Brooklyn was born, David's dad said to him, "You know, when you first look at your new-born baby, you'll understand how we feel about you." "Now I know what he meant," says David. "It's a wonderful feeling being a father. My mum absolutely loves babies, so she couldn't wait. My older sister's got a little girl and Victoria's sister Louise has a little girl too. Both sets of parents would love to have Brooklyn every day, but they've stood back and let us get on with looking after him. That's what we wanted because it's our first child, we've got to learn and it's nice that we can learn together."

But they're determined not to spoil him and will do all they can to bring up a well behaved child. "A lot of people have said, 'Oh Brooklyn's going to be a very spoilt little boy,' but I hate nasty children – I like very well behaved, polite children, and you don't have to have money to have those," says Victoria. "I had a lot of affection as a child and the only way he's going to be spoilt is with love. Obviously he's going to realise that his life is a bit different, but he's going to be a nice, polite little boy."

David feels he need look no further than his own parents as role models. "My mum and dad have always been there for me from day one," he says. "They've given me all the help and advice that I needed, but in the end they let me make the big decisions in my life. I think that's important because if you are pushed into something you go the other way."

Both David and Victoria are managing to combine their busy careers with parenthood. Says David: "Brooklyn and Victoria are the most important things in my life, but I am also dedicated to playing football and to Man Utd." Equally Victoria is committed to her career with the Spice Girls. "The baby will come with me wherever I work. The other girls in the group have been so relaxed about it," she says.

They may enjoy such trappings of success as flash cars, a luxurious home and designer clothes (they are both incredibly fashion conscious), but they insist that they are a normal couple. "Both of our families are really down-to-earth and we both are, too," says Victoria. "Our idea of a perfect Saturday night is at home with a take-away watching *Blind Date*. It really is. We both like watching *Friends* too. You won't see pictures of us coming out of clubs and pubs drunk, having spent the night with loads of famous people. That just isn't us."

David admits he was pretty uncool when he first met Victoria. She hunted him down, but he was so shy that he almost ruined any chance of a romance. "I went to see him in a football match because I liked him and I heard that he liked me. So I went to the match to hunt him down," Victoria laughs. "It's funny, because I'm really not into football at all. I mean, I go to the occasional game but I don't understand all the rules, off-side and all the rest of it – I only understand the goals. So afterwards

Above
David and Victoria like to take baby Brooklyn with them wherever they go, including shopping trips in London and Manchester.

"It's amazing how much you can love someone," says Victoria adoringly of Brooklyn.

when I met him in the players' lounge I didn't know what to say; what do you say – 'great game?'. So I probably said something naff like, 'Do you come here often?'" David laughs: "Do you come here often? – at Old Trafford!"

So what is his recollection? "The first time we met we just shook hands and smiled and looked at each other from opposite sides of the room. The second occasion, she came with Mel C. I went to the bar and then I heard this voice say, 'I'm just going to the bar Melanie'. I'm quite a shy person. I had a drink in each hand and I saw Victoria come over and I just said, 'Alright?' and walked away. I thought, 'I can't believe it. She came over to the bar and I walked away. I've missed my chance!' But we got chatting and ended up being the last ones in the lounge."

Says Victoria: "What I really liked was that David is really close to his family. They always go to his football matches and when I met him, he was standing with his mum, dad and sister." There was an instant attraction. And David felt the same way. "It was that feeling you have of wanting to be with someone, of wanting to make the effort to go and see them. I'd never had that before," he says.

They have built up an incredibly close relationship and hate being apart. "It's hard when we're away from each other – but in a way that's made us even stronger," says Victoria. "A lot of people would love to see us split up, without a doubt. David and I have both been accused of things but there's a trust between us, and as long as that's there, then it will always be the relationship it is."

It was David who first spotted the apartment when Victoria was on tour in America. "I was driving around and I saw these apartments and took a look at the penthouse," he says. "It was in a right state – it was a building site. We knocked lots of walls down to make bigger rooms." Even though she was across the Atlantic Victoria was very much involved. "I designed it all, picked out all the fabrics... My mum would come out to America with skirting board for me to look at!" she laughs. "I picked up lots of pieces from all over America, Europe too, and that's nice because walking round the house I'll see something and it reminds me of a certain place. There's a bit of a tribute to Mel G in the bedroom with all the leopard print!"

Seeing David at home, cradling Brooklyn in his arms, he looks the very picture of contentment and says he has put the trauma of being sent off during the World Cup behind him. "My way of getting away from everything that had gone on was going straight over to see Victoria. It was the first time I'd seen her since I knew she was pregnant, so it was important for me to get over to her," he says. "I needed support from Victoria but obviously she needed support from me as well. It was a special time and we wanted to be together."

"Once you meet that person that you want to spend your life with, you'd never hurt or destroy that relationship."

Right
The relationship has grown in strength, despite David and Victoria having to be apart a lot because of their busy careers.

Left
The huge white
sofa was worth
the trouble it
took getting it up
the various flights
of stairs!

Right
The master
bedroom is a place
of calm for the
couple – although
Brooklyn's nursery
is right next door.

"We're strong people – we know nothing will break us."

Above
The couple are
determined that no
amount of media
attention will
jeopardise their
family life.

Right
The harmonious
colours of their
home complement
the atmosphere
between David and
Victoria.

Weddings are often described as being "fairytale", but few come as genuinely close to that adjective as that of David and Victoria. The backdrop was like an enchanted forest – they exchanged vows in an ivy-clad folly, the bridesmaids dressed as fairies and there was even a castle. It took 14 months of meticulous planning and, despite calling in experts to help them, both David and Victoria were very much involved and had lots of ideas of their own.

Chapter 4

THE WEDDING

David and Victoria get married

Above

Bride and groom share a moment of tenderness at their wedding reception.

Victoria had told wedding organiser Peregrine Armstrong-Jones, whose company Bentley Entertainments had been responsible for Elton John's lavish 40th birthday bash, that she wanted somewhere unique that was green and leafy, deep in the countryside. He found the perfect setting for them in magnificent Luttrellstown Castle, a 14-bedroom property near Dublin, dating from 1794.

Set on a 560-acre estate with its own golf course, the castle is mainly the work of Henry Luttrell, second Earl of Carhampton. More recently it was home to Aileen Plunkett, daughter of Arthur Guinness of the famous Irish brewing family, who lived there until 1984. Surrounded by a high stone wall, it is becoming the choice of celebrities wishing to get away from it all. Last year Tom Cruise and Nicole Kidman hired the castle for a weekend.

Appropriate for such a leafy idyll, David and Victoria decided on a Robin Hood theme for the wedding, using plenty of greenery, twigs, and apples. Flowing fabric had three main colours: burgundy, dark green and cardinal purple. Typical of the attention to detail was the fresh apples, pierced to release their scent, that had been sewn into an ivy arrangement along the banisters of the master staircase. A beautiful, leafy walkway was created, stretching from the French windows of the library across the finely manicured lawns in front of the castle to a huge marquee where the reception and dancing would be held.

Most of the bride and groom's immediate family had been staying at the castle for the previous few days and had witnessed the transformation of the interior as carpets were meticulously brushed and huge floral arrangements were created in the major rooms. At around 3pm on 4 July, the two families gathered in the entrance hall of the castle and talked excitedly of their joy that all those months of preparation had finally come to fruition on the day.

"I still can't believe it," said Sandra Beckham, David's mother, who was dressed in a beautiful white suit by Frank Usher. "All the things we've talked about for months are actually here."

Right

Vera makes a sketch of Victoria on the rooftop of her New York studio as part of the fitting process.

Below

Victoria's hectic schedule had to be conducted by mobile phone during the fitting for her wedding dress.

Her husband Ted said he had never imagined his son's wedding day would be this spectacular. "It's just something special – a fairytale. Victoria's an absolutely lovely girl and I feel very, very proud of the pair of them." Football-mad Ted added that he also felt proud that Manchester United legend Sir Bobby Charlton was attending the wedding. "He was my absolute hero when I was a youngster," said Ted, "and my favourite moment was when I finally got to meet him, alongside David. He was everything I'd imagined he would be – and a bit more."

Victoria's father Tony, standing in his morning suit and cradling a top hat, admitted that the final few hours leading up to the wedding had made him very tearful. "I went into the marquee with Victoria earlier, the orchestra was rehearsing 'Goodbye' [a special version of the Spice Girls' Christmas 1998 hit] and I got so emotional that we had to have a little bit of a cuddle."

The arrival of the three bridesmaids, made up of Victoria's 22-year-old sister

Left
Victoria was very much involved in the design of the dress, including choice of colours and materials.

Below
Victoria's measurements had to be very precise, with Vera working on the dress in New York.

Vera is a perfectionist – she asked an Italian mill to dye the dress to make sure it precisely matched Victoria's specifications.

Right
Vera and her assistants discuss with Victoria her ideas for her dream wedding dress.

Louise, Louise's 13-month-old daughter, Liberty, plus David's niece, Georgina, 16 months, then caused a stir. The two little girls were dressed as woodland flower fairies in outfits made by theatrical costumiers Angels & Bermans, who worked closely with Victoria on the design. Attached to the back of their cream-coloured dresses were little gossamer wings, while wreaths of fake ivy were entwined around their wrists and ankles. On their heads they wore coronets decorated with ivy and twigs. Louise wore a dress by Chloe, the French design house now headed by Stella McCartney, which consisted of a fitted cream corset, laced at the back and decorated with copper and gold flowers and diamonds, with a long cream skirt.

All three bridesmaids had been presented with Tiffany diamond necklaces, as a wedding gift from David and Victoria. Best man, fellow Manchester United footballer Gary Neville, received a specially engraved Cartier watch, while usher Christian Adams, Victoria's brother, was given a gold and silver Rolex watch.

Then the remaining three Spice Girls arrived – Emma, Mel C and Mel G, with husband Jimmy Gulzar and baby Phoenix Chi. Emma wore an all-white ensemble of mini skirt, waistcoat, long morning coat and Homburg hat. Mel C was also in white – trousers, sleeveless top and trainers. Mel G wore a floor-length black dress with spaghetti straps. Colour themes had been dictated to all the guests: male guests had been asked to wear morning suits, while female guests should wear black, white, or a combination of both.

Despite the enormous publicity and anticipation that their wedding attracted, it was essentially a private occasion for the bride and groom's family and close friends. The Spice Girls completed the list of just 29 guests who had been invited to attend the ceremony at the tiny ivy-covered folly perched above a stream, just a five-minute drive through the castle woodlands.

As they waited for the fleet of Mercedes cars to transport them there, and also for the first glimpse of the bride, guests watched amused as little Liberty gleefully rolled around on the steps of the castle entrance, in her fairy costume. "Don't do that, Liberty," said Victoria's mum, Jackie, "you'll flatten your wings!"

The groom arrived, driving a silver convertible Bentley Azure worth £230,000, accompanied by Gary Neville, and they swept off towards the folly. The bride followed tradition by being a little late. At 4.05 pm, five minutes after the wedding ceremony was due to begin, Victoria swept into the entrance hall in her stunning wedding dress. As stylist Kenny Ho made the last few adjustments to her train, her smile was one of absolute happiness. The day and the moment for which she had waited so long was finally at hand.

In the months leading up to the wedding, everyone from fashion designers to newspaper columnists had been speculating about the style of her dress. In the event, she surprised everybody. Victoria described her simple champagne-coloured wedding dress, by American designer Vera Wang, as being "very

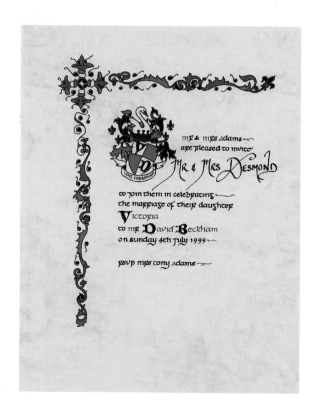

Above

Stylist Kenny Ho fits
Victoria into her
dress while Karin
Darnell, make-up
artist to the Spice
Girls, adds a touch
of lip gloss.

Left

The champagne-
coloured satin
dress, over a full
tulle petticoat, is
arranged perfectly
by Kenny.

"A lot of people were expecting me to have a tight little number with a great big slit up the side, but I wanted to look quite virginal on my wedding day."

Scarlett O'Hara". The fitted, strapless bodice, with a zip at the back, was made of Italian Clerici Duchess satin – the finest satin in the world. Underneath the full A-line skirt she wore a petticoat made of 50 metres of tulle which had been stiffened with horse hair. English corsetier Mr Pearl, who has been used by Christian Lacroix, Thierry Mugler and many of the other big couture houses in Paris, provided her with a tightly fitted corset.

Victoria had been a long-time admirer of Vera Wang, who has designed wedding dresses for such celebrities as Sharon Stone, Uma Thurman and Mariah Carey. Vera is a noted perfectionist, and only makes six to ten couture wedding dresses a year, with six to eight people working on each one. Victoria's own dress took two preliminary consultations, six fittings in New York and London, and fifteen months

Left and below

David beams with excitement as Kenny adjusts his cream cravat, then helps him into his jacket, designed by Timothy Everett.

to make. The finished product cleverly drew attention to her small waist.

On her feet, Victoria wore cream, high-heeled sandals of poidesoir satin with a 4-inch heel. A beautiful diamond and gold coronet by jeweller Slim Barrett, who made pieces for the Princess of Wales, adorned her head.

The bride's custom of wearing something old, new, borrowed and blue was adhered to. The something old was a diamond cross necklace that David bought her for Christmas last year, but which she had never worn because she was saving it for the wedding. The something new was the dress itself and pinned inside was a borrowed brooch that her mother and grandmother before her had worn inside their own wedding dresses. Small blue taffeta bows were also sewn inside her dress.

Victoria surprised guests with her bouquet which, in keeping with the theme, consisted of a natural selection of green berries, twigs, blackberries and brambles.

For their wedding jewellery, David and Victoria wore 18-carat yellow gold rings designed and made by Asprey and Garrard. Victoria's featured a stunning Marquise cut diamond, supported on each side by three grain set baguette diamonds. Each side of the shank of the ring was set with six diamonds. David wore an eternity ring, set with 24 baguette

Above

David's buttonhole followed through the theme of nature and woodland.

diamonds, with 24 smaller diamonds along one side of the shank. In addition, as a wedding gift, David gave Victoria a pair of emerald cut diamond earrings set in 18-carat yellow gold to match her wedding ring, and a gold waist chain with an Eternal cut diamond on one end. For David's gift, Victoria selected a beautiful Breguet wristwatch from Asprey and Garrard.

As family and friends were driven to the folly, the purple carpet stretching down the castle steps was given one last brush, a silver Bentley Arnage was manouvered into position, the imposing white doors of the castle were hauled open and Victoria stepped out into the sunshine and down into the waiting car.

Much work had gone into turning the folly into a fairy grotto that Victoria had envisaged. "It was a ruin and very cave-like when we found it, but Victoria loved the look of it," said Peregrine. "We had to do a tremendous amount of work to get

it ready for the day. Builders came in, put up scaffolding, laid a new floor and installed electrical power." The stone steps leading up to the entrance had been garlanded in ivy, woven with woodland flowers and ferns, forming a magical, leafy tunnel up to the main door. Inside, the walls and ceiling were covered in ivy and twinkling with tiny white lights.

A trumpet fanfare by pageanters positioned on the roof and dressed in traditional Irish costume sounded the bride's arrival. Inside, a string quartet had been entertaining the guests with classical pieces but at 4.32pm they launched into the melody everyone had been waiting for – "Here Comes The Bride" or, to give it its official title, the "Bridal Song" from Wagner's *Lohengrin*.

Victoria was escorted into the ceremony on the arm of her proud and clearly tearful father, Tony. At the altar, David, cradling the sleeping Brooklyn in his arms, smiled in wonder and sheer delight as he saw Victoria for the very first time in her beautiful dress. Baby Brooklyn was dressed in cream-coloured combat trousers, little cream boots and a cream shirt, which had his name embroidered on the back. A cream cowboy hat completed the ensemble.

Although all eyes were obviously directed towards the bride, David made sure that he looked equally as stylish. In a cream suit by English designer Timothy Everett, who also designs for Tom Cruise among others, David perfectly complemented the simplicity of Victoria's wedding gown. Under the knee-length jacket he wore a gold and cream waistcoat, cream shirt and cravat, and matching top hat and shoes. He also sported a diamond bracelet that Victoria had bought him from Cartier last year.

Above

Kenny, Karin and
Jennie Roberts,
Victoria's hair-
dresser, add
finishing touches
before the bride
enters the folly.

The Right Reverend Paul Colton, Bishop Of Cork, introduced the proceedings. In the background was the romantic sound of a stream tumbling over rocks below – and the less romantic purring of press helicopters in the distance, hoping to catch a glimpse of the event.

At the altar, David and Victoria exchanged glances and smiles and, after the first reading, David leaned across and kissed Victoria's right shoulder. After a short musical interlude of Tchaikovsky's "Song Without Words" the Right Reverend Colton began his address by repeating their names: "David and Victoria, Victoria and David. The marriage service doesn't give us a way of putting those names in order, but through your whole married life you put each other first."

Left and below
David and Victoria say their marriage vows before the Right Reverend Paul Colton, Bishop of Cork.

"There is a lot of interest in this marriage and we are all excited to be here," said the bishop. "But what matters is what is in David's heart and what is in Victoria's."

He continued that everything about the service, every sight and every sound, was beautiful. Then, referring to the helicopters overhead, he added: "apart from that particular noise", which drew smiles from those assembled. "But why do we do this?" he continued. "Why do we make everything so beautiful? It's simply because words fail us at a time like this. So we do all these beautiful things because they say better than words can: 'Thank you', and 'I love you'…"

He warned against empty infatuation by quoting an old Irish country priest: "The eyes that over cocktails seem so very sweet, may not seem so amorous over Shredded Wheat", which made Victoria smile. He then outlined his "three directions" for a successful marriage: good communication, caring for other people and finding a place for spirituality and for God in your lives.

Above

David gives Victoria her gold wedding ring as part of the ceremony that will make them man and wife.

The bride and groom turned to face the congregation as the banns were called: "If anyone knows any cause or just impediment why these two should not be joined together" – and the Bishop placed the couple's hands over each other before beginning the marriage vows.

David Robert Joseph Beckham and Victoria Caroline Adams were officially declared man and wife and there was a whoop from one of the congregation followed by cheers and applause. Victoria and David laughed, smiled and then kissed, still clutching each other's hands. They then knelt at the altar as prayers were said. "Almighty God, giver of life and love; Bless Victoria and David whom you have now joined in marriage. Grant them wisdom and devotion in their life together." At just before 5pm, the orchestra struck up Mendelssohn's "Wedding March" and the service ended.

Back at the castle, guests walked up an impressive staircase which was covered with a rich purple carpet. At this stage, the remainder of the 226 guests also arrived, to be greeted by pageanters in Irish costume, playing a fanfare on the castle battlements, while six-foot silk flames shot out of the turrets. A purple flag flew, decorated with David and Victoria's specially designed crest, which also featured on the wedding invitations. Once inside, they could not help but marvel at the elegant surroundings of the wedding venue. They were greeted by a 15-foot tall

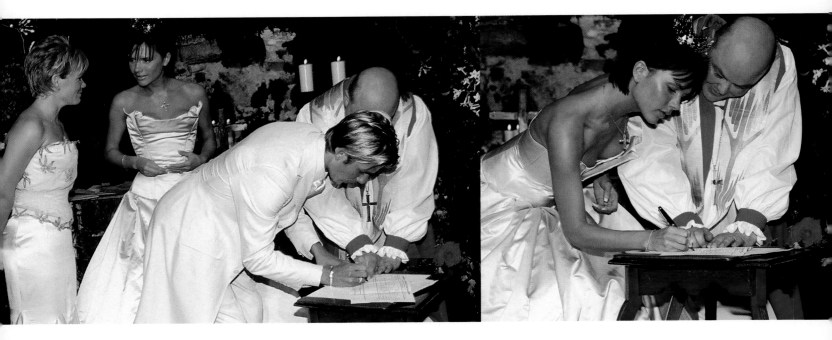

column bursting with a floral arrangement of red roses, purple flowers and a plethora of greenery.

Inside the castle, a pianist helped create the elegant atmosphere while the Spice Girls, Victoria and David's family, and the rest of the assembled guests sipped on Laurent Perrier pink champagne, elderflower cordial with raspberries and Sicilian red orange juice. They also nibbled on canapés, which included Asian chicken skewers served with an orange dipping sauce, miniature leek and cheese tartlets topped with tomato and red onion salsa, baby potatoes with a cream horseradish sauce, flaked lobster and salmon on a baby French croute topped with caviar.

Everyone at the reception agreed that the ceremony was beautiful. "It was lovely," said Victoria's sister Louise. David's sister Joanne said: "It was so emotional. All of us were in tears, including Victoria and David."

The happy couple made a spectacular entrance down the 18th-century staircase, adorned with a swathe of flowers and apples, while a pianist played the theme tune from *Beauty and the Beast*. They love listening to the Disney soundtracks and this is one of their favourites. "No doubt people will be wondering which one of us is Beauty and which one the Beast," Victoria had laughed the day before her wedding.

Everyone then made their way to the reception marquee, attached to the castle by a 250-metre walkway decorated in a swathe of birch trees and reeds which had been woven into mats to make a thatched covering. Lights were entwined into it with ferns and ivy.

The marquee itself was carpeted in a sumptuous deep red carpet and the walls lined with pleated ivory taffeta. Spectacular flower arrangements of burgundy, green and purple created a suitably regal effect. The tables themselves were covered in dark green velvet, overlaid in cream-coloured Irish calico, trimmed with purple. Beautiful table decorations of apples, greenery and candles created a very organic effect. One of Victoria's own ideas was to cover a wall with birch trees and different foliages to make it look like the waiters were coming out of a forest. The lighting

Above

David and then Victoria sign the wedding register, witnessed by Victoria's sister and Gary Neville.

Right

Mr and Mrs David Beckham.

was also made to fit in with the back-to-nature decor, with moss-coloured candles and two huge chandeliers, draped with foliage and apples, fitted with tiny twinkling lights. Ten-foot-high Regency glass windows built into the marquee, draped with cream voiles, gave a view of the castle and the floodlit grounds.

But nobody could take their eyes off the main attraction in the marquee, the bride and groom, who were seated on throne-like chairs on a dais in their own "bridal alcove", lined with luxuriant Irish green crushed velvet. Brooklyn, who was not to be outdone by his parents, was placed in his favourite swinging chair, decorated in burgundy velvet with gold ribbons.

The magnificent dinner was suitably lavish for the grandeur of the occasion. Some months before the wedding, Victoria and David had personally conducted a

Above

David and Victoria's parents proudly pose alongside their famous wedded offspring.

taste test of dozens of different dishes to decide what they wanted to include on their wedding menu. They settled on roasted red pepper and tomato soup served in hollowed out pumpkin halves instead of plates. This was followed by a corn-fed chicken with English asparagus, roast potatoes, and a French bean and sugar snap medley. For the vegetarian guests, chef Jason Reynolds conjured up deep fried Irish Brie with sage, served with cranberry sauce. For dessert, Victoria and David had chosen two puddings for the gentlemen and ladies: the men were treated to David's favourite, sticky toffee pudding with butterscotch; the women were given summer berry terrine with summer fruits in a brandy snap basket with raspberry coulis.

As the guests enjoyed the meal, an 18-piece string orchestra, seated on a 10-foot tall mezzanine draped in white voile, played a selection of Spice Girls hits including "Say You'll Be There", "Mama" and "Two Become One", as well as standard melodies such as "Cheek To Cheek" and "Night And Day".

Just before 10.30pm the Master of Ceremonies rose and announced the cutting of the cake, a lavish three-tier creation by Rachel Mount, featuring one tier of

Right

Best man Gary
Neville gives
Victoria a
congratulatory kiss
on the cheek after
the ceremony.

traditional fruit cake, one tier of vanilla sponge and one of carrot cake. The entire cake was smothered in green and purple leaves, made of icing, while the supporting pillars for each tier were made of red apples. Sitting on the top was a fondant sculpture of an almost naked David, Victoria and Brooklyn! The couple cut the cake using a silver sword, which had been made especially for them as a gift from Brooklyn. It was engraved with the couple's crest and an inscription from their son.

Victoria's father Tony then stood for his speech: "Ladies and gentlemen, many people would like to be here today but it is you that David and Victoria have chosen. It is with great pride that I speak to you for a few moments about our bride and groom." He said that Victoria, the eldest of their three children, had never been any trouble as a child: "She started dance classes at the age of three and was soon rushing home from school to change from her uniform into a leotard to kick her legs about. Little did she know that just a few miles away there was a little boy changing from his uniform into shorts to kick a ball around. They continued with enthusiasm and at 16 both left home to continue their training. Victoria went to dance college in Epsom and we all know where David went. As it happened, they both did quite well!"

Right
Victoria is very close to her brother Christian and sister Louise, here with Louise's daughter Liberty.

Below
Victoria enjoys a hug with her close friend, the television presenter Dani Behr.

84
THE
WEDDING

Left

David and Victoria
pose with her
fellow Spice Girls,
Melanie Chisholm,
Melanie Gulzar and
Emma Bunton.

He went on to tell the story of how David had seen a girl from an all-girl group on television and had said: "That's the girl I'm going to marry." Tony joked: "Unfortunately, he was talking about Louise from Eternal, and Jamie Redknapp got there first!" Tony also told how David had found out which clubs Victoria went to in London and came down hoping to meet her, and how the pair had finally got together after Victoria and Melanie Chisholm went to Old Trafford: "Where their eyes met across a crowded players' lounge. The rest, as they say, is history."

Paying tribute to the couple, he said: "This afternoon I have given David someone who is very precious to me but I know he will look after her, as he always does, with the utmost love and affection. We know we couldn't wish for a better son-in-law." He finished by asking guests to be upstanding and to join his wife Jackie and himself in wishing "our bride and groom a life of love and happiness. To the rest of the world they are Posh and Becks. But to us they are David and Victoria."

When David took to the microphone he received a huge cheer as he thanked their guests for coming on behalf of "my wife and I." He then continued: "I'm sure you'll all agree that the bridesmaids looked absolutely beautiful and stunning and I'd like to say that our mums have scrubbed up very well today too! My mother- and father-in-law have loved and supported me and obviously that means the world to me. Jackie and Tony have given me something very precious to them. I will always love and look after Victoria and treat her like a princess – which she always wants to be treated like."

Above

The entire Manchester United team took time out from their busy schedules to share the day with David and Victoria.

Right

Victoria looking radiant in her exquisite bridal gown, holding her bouquet of apples, berries and foliage.

David then turned to Victoria's brother and said: "Christian, I've always wanted a brother and that's how I feel about you. And I feel just as close to Louise. I'd also like to thank my mum and dad who have brought me up from a young age – obviously! – and my sisters, who have been there from day one – obviously! Also, my nan and grandad who, in a few weeks will be celebrating their 50th wedding anniversary. I love you!

Referring to his best man, he added: "If Gary Neville's performances have been a bit shaky in the last few months, now you know why. He's been disappearing off to the toilet, wiping his brow and looking very worried. But Gary has always been there for me when I've needed him – especially when Victoria was away, and I needed someone to talk to. I'd like to say that I really love you Gary, and you'll notice that we kiss a lot on the pitch!"

He finished by paying tribute to his new wife and to his son Brooklyn: "This has been a massive year for us but she couldn't have given me a better present than the one she presented me with four months ago. Victoria wakes up every day and she seems to get more beautiful every time I see her. I know that a lot of people say that we've done it the wrong way round – had Brooklyn and then got married – but if you've got love, nothing else matters."

Finally came the best man, Gary Neville. As David re-took his seat next to Victoria, Gary said: "He speaks well that Julian Clary, doesn't he?" He went on to thank the staff at the castle and at the marquee, Paul Colton, the Bishop of Cork, those who helped organise the wedding and David and Victoria's "active role" in the whole event. Gary then said that he would read out some of the telegrams from

"I think love is a very strong word and all my love goes to Victoria and Brooklyn."

guests who could not make the ceremony. "The first is from Diego Simeone," said Gary – and held up a red card! On the stage, David burst out laughing. Alex Ferguson, who was attending another wedding, sent a telegram saying: "Dear David and Victoria, sorry we cannot be there to share your special day, but we would like to take this opportunity of wishing you both every happiness as you start out on married life."

Gary added: 'People are always asking me why I always kiss David Beckham. My answer is that I'd usually do more than that to a six-foot blonde in shorts with legs up to their armpits!" He gave his version of how David and Victoria had met and said that David had been "besotted" with her from the first moment. "He would come into training every day like a little schoolboy – you'd go a long way to find two people more in love." He said that Victoria looked "absolutely beautiful" and that "Brooklyn and Victoria have made David the happiest person in the world. That, in turn, has made me happy and everyone else here in the room. Ladies and gentlemen, enjoy the evening and drink away!"

Above and right
After David's speech, the couple cut their wedding cake with a silver sword – a gift from their son Brooklyn.

Left
David and Victoria were the obvious centre of attention, seated on plush thrones on their own raised dais.

After the speeches, guests were given coffee and petit fours which included orange zest coated in dark chocolate, nougat dipped in chocolate, and a hazelnut praline log. The bride and groom then lead their guests through to a second marquee, decorated in sumptuous Moroccan style, with luxuriant purple and gold drapes and huge gold statues bearing towering floral arrangements. The sunken dance floor was painted in a black and white chequerboard design and surrounded by comfy chaise longues and huge velvet and leopard print cushions, with low level tables topped with silver dishes of bon bons.

At this point, the bride and groom slipped away to change into their evening attire, designed by their friend Antonio Beradi. Victoria wore what she described as a "Jessica Rabbit dress" – a slim fitting, strapless, fishtailed dress of purple stretched satin, with a thigh-length split and bright red lining, which matched her red nail polish. A wreath of handmade silk flowers, dusted with tiny crystals that twinkled like dew drops when the light caught them, trailed over one shoulder. Strappy silver sandals by Manolo Blahnik completed the outfit.

David, his hair now in a quiff, wore a matching purple suit, which consisted of a double-breasted jacket with a red lining and purple wing-collared shirt and waistcoat. The trousers, slightly flared at the ankle, were teamed with purple suede shoes. Brooklyn too had changed into a purple outfit to match his parents – an exact copy of the Antonio Beradi ensemble he had been sporting earlier in the day.

Then it was time to dance the night away to music from the sixties and seventies, sprinkled with salsa, from DJ Hugo Fuller, alternated with a live soul band formed especially for the occasion by the Spice Girls' musical director David Laudant.

At two o'clock, guests gathered on a huge balcony, built onto one side of the marquee and decorated entirely in black, save for a drinks bar covered in zebra print, and dominated by a huge Egyptian-style cat sculpture. From here they were able to watch the evening's spectacular finale – a four-and-a-half minute firework display, accompanied by Björk's atmospheric hit "Hush". When the last firework had lit the black sky, the guests went to their beds, safe in the knowledge that they had witnessed the wedding of the decade.

Left

Following wedding tradition, David and Victoria led the first dance of the evening as bride and groom.

Right

The walkway to the dancefloor had an exotic, Moroccan feel to blend with the couple's evening outfits.

Below

A spectacular firework display marked the end of the evening, and the wedding of the decade.

First published in the United Kingdom in 1999 by
NORTHERN & SHELL PLC, proprietors of OK! Magazine, in
association with CASSELL & CO

This is an official OK! publication. It is not offically
endorsed by David Beckham or Victoria Adams

Photographs: All Action 4 *b*, 18, 19, 26, 37, 53*b*, 54*m* & *br*,
57; All Sport 16*r*, 17*l*, 21, 23, 25; BICI 56; Big Pictures 52*l*;
Brian Aris © OK! Magazine, 1, 2, 5*t* & *br*, 28–9, 31, 42, 43,
44, 45, 46, 48–9, 51, 59, 60, 61, 62–96; Camera Press 5*bl*,
17*r*, 24, 38, 39*t*, 54*bl*; John Jones 12, 13, 14; Katz 8–9, 11, 36,
40, 41; Doug Peters 53*l*; Rex Features 22, 52*r*, 54*t*, 55*r*; LFI
16*l*, 35, 39*b*, 55*l*; Gay Soper 32; Frank Spooner 34

A CIP catalogue record for this book is available from the
British Library

ISBN 8 304 353833

Designed by Nigel Soper
Edited by Zoë Ross
Typset in Bembo
Printed and bound in England by Butler & Tanner Ltd,
Frome and London

Northern & Shell plc
The Northern & Shell Tower
City Harbour
London
E14 9GL